A
WAS ONCE AN
APPLE PIE

Chill Out with a good book!

To PRE TODDLERS

From THE MADSEN FAMILY

SCHOLASTIC

A B C D
E F G H I
J K L M

N O P Q R

S T U V

W X Y Z

ORCHARD BOOKS

AN IMPRINT OF SCHOLASTIC INC. • NEW YORK

EDWARD LEAR'S

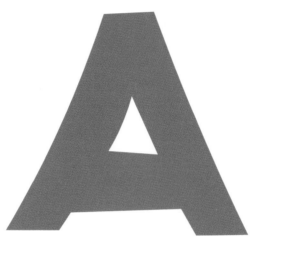

A

WAS ONCE AN APPLE PIE

ADAPTED AND ILLUSTRATED BY

SUSE MACDONALD

A

was once an apple pie,

pidy, widy, tidy, pidy,

nice insidy, apple pie!

B

was once a little bear,

beary, wary, hairy, beary,

taky cary, little bear!

C was once a little cat,
catty, batty, matty, catty,
furry, fatty, little cat!

D was once a little dog,

doggy, moggy, oggy, noggy,

waggy, woggy, little dog!

E was once a little eel,
eely, weely, peely, eely,
twirly, tweely, little eel!

F

was once a little fish,

fishy, squishy, dishy, fishy,

make a wishy, little fish!

 was once a little goose,

goosey, moosey, boosey, goosey,

waddley, woosey, little goose!

H

was once a little hen,
henny, chenny, tenny, henny,
eggsy-any, little hen?

I

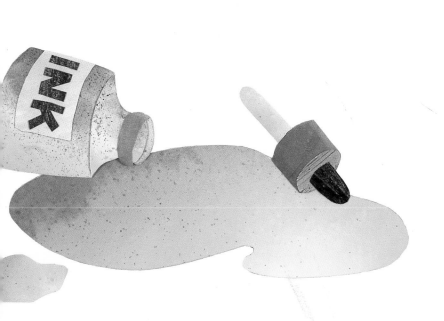

was once a bottle of ink,
inky, dinky, thinky, inky,
plunky, plinky, bottle of ink!

was once a little jay,
jady, mady, dady, jady,
in the shady, little jay!

K

was once a little kite,
kity, whity, flighty, kity,
out of sighty, little kite!

L

was once a little lark,
larky, marky, harky, larky,
in the parky, little lark!

 was once a little mouse,

mousey, bousey, blousey, mousey,

where's your housey, little mouse?

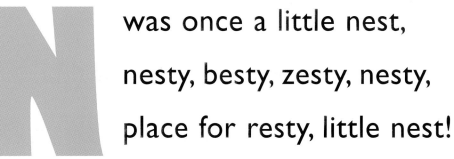

N was once a little nest,
nesty, besty, zesty, nesty,
place for resty, little nest!

O was once a little owl,
owly, prowly, howly, owly,
browny fowly, little owl!

P was once a little pig,
piggy, wiggy, jiggy, piggy,
plump and biggy, little pig!

Q was once a little quail,
quaily, faily, daily, quaily,
by the raily, little quail!

R was once a little rose,
rosy, posy, nosy, rosy,
blowsy, growsy, little rose!

S

was once a little skunk,

skunky, dunky, chunky, skunky,

stinky, stunky, little skunk!

T

was once a turkey tom,

turkey, lurkey, perky, turkey,

herky-jerky, turkey tom!

U
was once a unicorn,
uni, tunie, junie, uni,
see you soonie, unicorn!

V

was once a little vine,
viny, winy, twiny, viny,
twisty, twiny, little vine!

W

was once a whale,

whaly, scaly, shaly, whaly,

tumbly taily, mighty whale!

X was once a hefty ox,

oxy, boxy, loxy, oxy,

full of moxie, hefty ox!

 was once a little yak,

yacky, wacky, tacky, yacky,

backy-packy, little yak!

Z

was once a little zebra,
zeebie, deebie, heebie, jeebie,
weebie, meebie, little zebra!

A B C D
E F H
G I
TO PATTI ANN
J K
L M

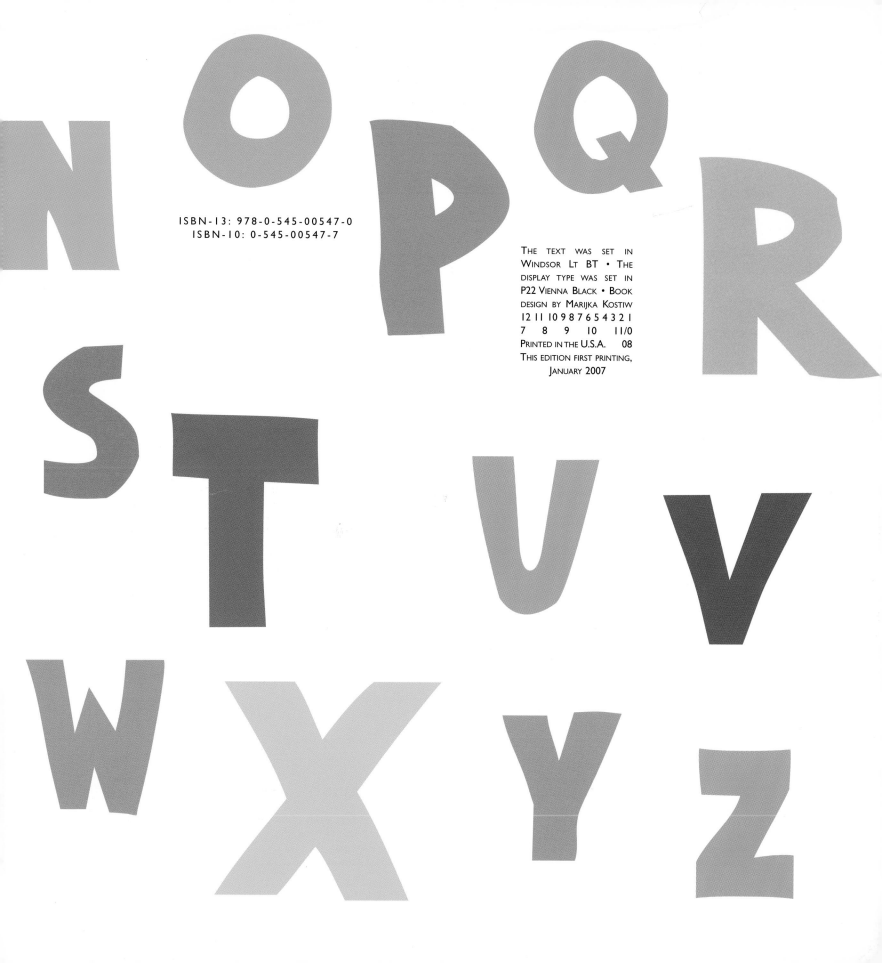

ISBN-13: 978-0-545-00547-0
ISBN-10: 0-545-00547-7

THE TEXT WAS SET IN
WINDSOR LT BT • THE
DISPLAY TYPE WAS SET IN
P22 VIENNA BLACK • BOOK
DESIGN BY MARIJKA KOSTIW
12 11 10 9 8 7 6 5 4 3 2 1
7   8   9   10   11/0
PRINTED IN THE U.S.A.   08
THIS EDITION FIRST PRINTING,
JANUARY 2007